To Alice,

Well done for first prize in the smoothie project competition.

Mrs Hamson

CW00497495

# smoothies

## 101 Delicious Smoothies

A smoothie is a delicious and nutritious drink made up of blended fruit and or vegetables. Traditionally, smoothies are considered healthy drinks as the basic ingredients are typically packed with the vitamins and nutrients needed to maintain a healthy balanced diet, and in their most basic form they are an excellent way of ensuring that we eat lots of fruit and vegetables. They are also a great way of making sure that kids receive essential nutrients, as many smoothies look pretty yummy when made - not unlike milkshakes!

By creating your own smoothies, you may have to invest a little time, but you will in the long term save yourself money - even if you have to buy equipment to begin with.  And for those times when you fancy something that is naughty as well as nice we have included a few indulgent recipes - and even a few that contain alcohol (these are clearly marked).

To grab a smoothie on the go, make them up ahead of time. You can freeze a smoothie and thaw it out when you want it but remember that you'll need to allow some space in the container because your smoothie will likely expand when freezing.

The only equipment that you really need to make a smoothie is a blender. Smoothie making is very simple, but here are some tips and ideas to keep in mind.  The first step in making a smoothie is assembling your ingredients and there are four different categories of ingredients that you can use:

## Liquids

These help to give your smoothie a thinner, drinkable consistency. Add the liquids to the blender first, to prevent it from binding up on the frozen fruit and getting stuck.

Fruit Juice

Any fruit juice works great; try squeezing the juice of an orange or lemon for a fresh flavour.

Milk

Using skimmed milk or soy milk adds protein and a creamy flavour and is also a healthier option than full fat milk.

Water

Plain water is sometimes the best option, especially if you have a lot of flavours going on with the other ingredients.

## Solid ingredients

These often make up the bulk of your smoothie, and for this category you will often have more than one of the following:

Yoghurt — Plain yoghurt is ideal if you are adding in your own fruit, since the fruit-infused yoghurts have hidden added sugars.

Fresh Fruits — Any fresh fruit — peaches, pears, mangos, and more — can be added to a smoothie; just remove any seeds and skin and toss into the blender. (See back of book for nutritional value of fruits).

Tofu — A smoothie with tofu will have added protein, which is important especially if you are drinking the smoothie for a meal; choose the silken kind as it is much creamier than the firm varieties.

Peanut Butter — This will add healthful fats and protein and great flavour, especially delicious with bananas.

**Fruits or Vegetables**

The recipes don't always specify, but if you have time to freeze your fruit beforehand, your smoothie will stay colder and be thicker than if your fruit is warm.

Large fruits (like bananas or melons) should be chopped into pieces before freezing. Spread the pieces on a plate or baking sheet while in the freezer which will make sure the fruit doesn't freeze in one big unmanageable lump. Once frozen, then you can store them together in a freezer bag or container. Using frozen strawberries, blueberries, or even mixed berries will add a sweet and slightly tart flavour.

## Flavour Add-ins

These can pull all the flavours in the smoothie together and provide a "kick"; as an added bonus, the following also add a nutritional punch:

*Cinnamon* Any spice, including cinnamon, can add flavour as well as boost the nutritional properties of your smoothie.

*Ginger* Either freshly grated or powdered ginger will add a great spicy flavour to the smoothie.

*Mint* Fresh herbs such as mint or parsley give smoothies a fresh flavour. Just give a rough chop before tossing into the blender.

**Berry Berry Smoothie** (serves 2)

2 kiwis, peeled and cut into 4 pieces
1 banana
5 strawberries
7 raspberries
335g/1 1/2 cup low fat natural yoghurt
1 medium size glass milk

## Method

Put all ingredients in the blender, blend until desired consistency, serve immediately.
If you think it is too thick, just add more milk.

**Berry Bonanza Smoothie** (serves 2)

20 blueberries
20 strawberries
2 mangos
25ml/3 teaspoons pure apple juice

## Method

Cut the mangos up into small pieces then add to blender. Next add the apple juice,
blueberries and strawberries. Blend until smooth. For a more creamier and colder
version, try adding a little bit of vanilla ice cream to the mix.

**Berry Burst Smoothie** (serves 2)

1 handful of raspberries
1 chopped mango
1 lime (juice only)
2 peeled oranges
splash of apple juice
6 ice cubes

## Method

Blend together your mango, oranges and raspberries. Then add your lime juice and splash of apple juice, blend again. Finally add your ice, blend until cubes are crushed.

**Berry Delight Smoothie** (serves 2)

150ml/2/3 cup raspberry yoghurt
75ml/1/3 cup natural yoghurt
50ml/3 tablespoons milk
50g/1/2 cup frozen raspberries
2 pears peeled, cored and chopped

## Method

Blend all ingredients for 30 seconds until smooth, keeping a little of the natural yoghurt aside to dribble on top of your finished smoothie.

**Berry Refresher**  (serves 2)
2 bananas
115g/1 cup of raspberries
60g/1/2 cup frozen blueberries
10-12 frozen strawberries
225-450ml/1-2 cups cranberry juice

Method

Place all ingredients in a blender
and blend until smooth.

**Berry-Tastic Smoothie** (serves 1)
1 handful of blueberries
3 plums
1/2 glass of cranberry juice
4 tablespoons of Greek yoghurt
1 banana
4-5 ice cubes

Method

Remove the stone from the plums and roughly
chop them and place in the blender. Add the
blueberries, banana, cranberry juice, greek yoghurt,
then the ice.

**Berry Tropical Fruit Smoothie** (serves 4)
2 apples
6 large strawberries
1 large cup of berries
1 large cup of chopped/cubed pineapple
1 medium cup of ice (cubed or crushed)
1 medium cup of fresh orange juice
1 pot of natural yoghurt

## Method

Put everything in the blender and blast on the highest speed. The ice makes it cold and the yoghurt adds flavour and makes it creamy.

**Berry and Vodka Smoothie** (serves 1)                    **Alcoholic**
6 cherries, 6 strawberries and 6 raspberries
110ml/1/2 cup lemon lime soda
1 peach
12 grapes
1 banana
100ml/3 1/2fl oz vodka

## Method

Roughly chop the fruit, add to blender. Pour in the lemon lime soda and vodka (add ice if preferred). Blend. This can also be made without the vodka.

**Blackberry Icecream Smoothie** (serves 2)
60g/1/2 cup blackberries (fresh or frozen)
110ml/1/2 cup vanilla ice cream
1/2 banana
110ml/1/2 cup milk

## Method

Blend the milk with the banana and and blackberries until a slushy texture is formed. Add ice cream for extra sweetness and blend till smooth.

**Blackberry and Cherry Smoothie** ( serves 2)

115g/1 cup cherries
60g/1/2 cup of blackberries
1 large glass of water

Method

Place ingredients in the blender and blend until smooth.

**Blackberry and Honeydew Melon Smoothie** (serves 2)

230g/2 cups of frozen blackberries
230g/2 cups honeydew melon (fresh or frozen)
40g/1/3 cup of sugar (or more to taste)

Method

Puree all ingredients in a blender. Blend. Pour and serve.

**Blissful Berries Smoothie** (serves 2)
115g/1 medium cup of raspberries
115g/1 medium cup of strawberries
1 banana
450ml/2 cups of orange juice

## Method

Put all the fruit and juice into the blender, then blend until smooth.

**Blueberry Blast Smoothie** (serves 2)
110ml/1/2 cup of skimmed milk
225g/1 cup of low fat vanilla ice cream
230g/2 cups of frozen blueberries

## Method

Put all ingredients in the blender and blend until smooth.

**Blueberry and Blackcurrant Burst Smoothie** (serves 2)
250g/2 cups fresh blackcurrants
125g/1 cup blueberries
1 teaspoon of honey or sugar (optional)

## Method

Place all ingredients in a blender with 6 ice cubes. Blend. Pour and serve.

**Blackberry, Cherry and Apple Pie Smoothie** (serves 2)
approx 20 cherries
1 apple
1 banana
1 kiwi
1 handful of blueberries
cloudy apple juice

## Method

Stone the cherries and put into the blender. Add the chopped apple, banana, kiwi and blueberries. Blend with a splash of apple juice to loosen.

**Mixed Berry Madness Smoothie** (serves 2)
1/2 cup of frozen mixed berries
1/2 ltr/2 1/4 cups apple juice
2 tablespoons of honey
1 tablespoon of natural yoghurt

## Method

Add mixed berries to blender, then add apple juice, honey and yoghurt. Blend until smooth. Serve and enjoy.

**Cinnamon Surprise Smoothie** (serves 2)
2 bananas
1 small cup of frozen raspberries
1 small cup of frozen blueberries
1 small cup of pure orange juice
1 teaspoon vanilla essence
1 teaspoon maple syrup
3 ice cubes
cinnamon to taste

## Method

Place all ingredients in the blender and blend until smooth. The more cinnamon added the more delicious it is.

**Cranberry Smoothie** (serves 1)
225g/1 cup cranberry juice, chilled
6 medium strawberries, hulls removed and cut into halves
1/2 banana, cut into quarters
110ml/1/2 cup crushed ice

## Method

Put all ingredients in a blender. Blend for a few seconds on high speed or until all of the ingredients are thoroughly combined.

**Cranberry and Orange Squeeze Smoothie** (serves 2)

225ml/1 cup cranberry juice
110ml/1/2 cup sorbet, raspberry flavour
1 tablespoon orange juice concentrate
60g/1/2 cup of orange segments
60g/1/2 cup fresh cranberries, or cherries (if preferred)

Method

Combine the cranberry juice, sorbet, and orange juice concentrate in
a blender. Add the orange sections and cranberries. Blend until smooth.

**Cranberry and Strawberry Smoothie** (serves 2)

225ml/8fl oz cranberry juice
5 strawberries cut into halves
5 ice cubes

Method

Place all ingredients into blender, and process until smooth.

**Raspberry Protein Smoothie** (serves 2)
60g/1/2 cup frozen unsweetened raspberries
40g/1/3 cup oats
1 tablespoon fat-free vanilla yoghurt
110ml/1/2 cup skimmed milk
2 tablespoons vanilla or chocolate powder (optional)

## Method

Firstly blend ice, milk and yoghurt together. Next add the powder (optional) and oats, blend again. Then add raspberries and pulse several times to make sure it is mixed well.

**Raspberry Ripple Smoothie** (serves 2)
1 medium banana
60g/1/2 cup of red raspberries (or strawberries)
60g/1/2 cup of blackberries (or blueberries)
110g/1/2 cup of yoghurt
110ml/1/2 cup of ice

## Method

Cut the raspberries into small pieces that will fit through a straw. Blend the banana, ice, and yoghurt with the blackberries. Layer alternating chopped raspberries and smoothies through the glass.

**Raspberry and Lemon Smoothie** (serves 1)

15 raspberries

lemonade - a good splash (should not cover the raspberries)

## Method

Place raspberries in the blender, pour over some lemonade (making sure you don't cover them). Blend for approximately 20 seconds, serve and enjoy.

**Raspberry and Orange Tang Smoothie** (serves 2)

10 raspberries

juice squeezed from 5 oranges

50ml/1 2/3fl oz still water

50ml/1 2/3fl oz cranberry juice

## Method

Place raspberries in the blender first, then add the freshly squeezed orange juice. Blend for 10-15 seconds. Add cranberry juice and water. Mix on high for 8 more seconds.

Tip: This smoothie has more of a juice consistency than being a thick smoothie consistency, so if you prefer it to be thicker just add less or no water.

**Raspberry and Peach Soft Smoothie** (serves 2)
275g/10oz frozen raspberries (slightly thawed)
225ml/1 cup peach juice
110ml/1/2 cup buttermilk
1 tablespoon of honey

## Method

Place all ingredients into blender, and process until smooth.

**Raspberry Margarita Smoothie**  (serves 2)                    **Alcoholic**
15-20 raspberries
2 cups of crushed ice
150ml/2/3 cup margarita mixer
2 shots tequilla
1 tablespoon orange juice concentrate
2 teaspoons sweetened lime juice

## Method

Put raspberries in a blender, then add margarita mixer, tequilla, orange juice concentrate and sweetened lime juice, add crushed ice on top. Blend until nearly smooth. Pour into 2 glasses and garnish with whole raspberries.

**Triple Berry Smoothie** (serves 2)
60g/1/2 cup blueberries
60g/1/2 cup raspberries
1 banana
110g/1/2 cup yoghurt
225ml/1 cup milk
110ml/1/2 cup ice cubes

## Method

Blend the banana, ice, yoghurt, milk, and other berries together until
a smooth drink is formed. Pour into a cup and enjoy a very fruity,
healthy smoothie.

**Very Berry Smoothie** (serves 2)
Ingredients
30g/1/4 cup of blueberries
30g/1/4 cup of raspberries
1 large banana
100ml/3 1/2fl oz of low fat berry yoghurt, orange juice and ice

## Method

Place all ingredients in mixer. Blend for approximately 30 seconds.

**Banana Smoothie** (serves 3)
55ml/1/4 cup orange juice
4 bananas
3 scoops of plain ice cream
2 tablespoons of golden syrup
3 tablespoons of plain yoghurt
lemon juice (optional)
sugar (optional)

## Method

Cut the bananas into small pieces and put in the blender. Add all the other ingredients. Blend on full for 20 seconds. Put lemon juice around the rim of the glasses then roll the rim in the sugar so it sticks to the lemon juice.

**Banana and Apple Smoothie** (serves 1)
1 whole banana, chopped into 4 pieces
1 whole apple, peeled and chopped into 4 pieces
110ml/1/2 cup of pure orange juice
55ml/1/4 cup low fat milk

## Method

Place all ingredients in the blender for approximately 20 seconds.

**Banana Berry Smoothie** (serves 2)

1 banana

110g/1/2 cup of low fat vanilla yoghurt

60g/1/2 cup of frozen peaches

115g/1 cup of frozen strawberries

1 tablespoon of orange juice concentrate

## Method

Roughly chop the banana, then place all ingredients in the blender, (add ice if preferred to fill blender), blend until smooth.

**Banana & Blackberry Smoothie** (serves 2)

2 chopped bananas

200ml/7/8 cup milk

200g/3/4 cup Greek yoghurt, chilled

1 tablespoon clear honey

250g/2 cups fresh blackberries

Extra banana, yoghurt and blackberries to serve, optional

## Method

Blend all of the ingredients together for approximately 20 seconds. Place a spoonful of yoghurt in the base of 2 serving glasses and add a few blackberries and slices of banana then add the smoothie and serve.

**Banana Blitz Smoothie** (serves 2)

1 banana
115g/1 cup of frozen strawberries
6 ice cubes
banana essence flavouring

## Method

Put the strawberries, banana (chopped) and ice into the blender. Blend for about 30 seconds. Then add a dash of banana flavouring (any kind) and blend until smooth.

**Banana Boogie Smoothie** (serves 2)

1 medium sized banana
honey flavoured yoghurt (add according to taste)
2 teaspoons honey
1/2 mug of milk

## Method

Place all ingredients into a blender (leave a couple of slices of banana for later). Mix for 10 seconds at low speed, then mix again for 5 seconds at high speed. Serve into glasses and put the banana slices which you left to one side on the rim of each glass. Serve, drink and enjoy.

**Banana and Blueberry Smoothie** (serves 2)
60g/1/2 cup of blueberries
1 banana
2 tablespoons of vanilla yoghurt
110ml/1/2 small cup of milk (skimmed or full fat)
1 scoop of vanilla ice cream

Method

Place all ingredients in the blender, mix for 30 seconds or till smooth.

**Banana Breakfast Smoothie** (serves 2)
2 peaches
2 bananas chopped
225g/8oz can of crushed/chopped pineapple
75ml/1/3 cup of chopped mango
225ml/1 cup of low fat milk

Method

Place all ingredients into a blender, then blitz till smooth.

**Banana Burst Smoothie** (serves 1)
1 chopped banana
1 medium sized cup of any berry (strawberry/raspberry etc)
1 egg white
1 tablespoon of honey

1/2 small cup of any yoghurt (natural is good)
6 ice cubes

## Method

Add all ingredients into blender and blend until smooth. Serve and enjoy.

**Banana and Cherry Smoothie** (serves 2)
1 banana, chopped into 4
130g/1 cup of sweet cherries (pitted and stem removed)
juice from 1/2 lemon
110g/1/2 cup of low-fat plain yoghurt
5 cubes of ice
2 drops of almond extract (optional)

## Method

Put all ingredients in the blender and blend until
smooth. Should you require a hint of
almond, then add the drops
of almond extract.

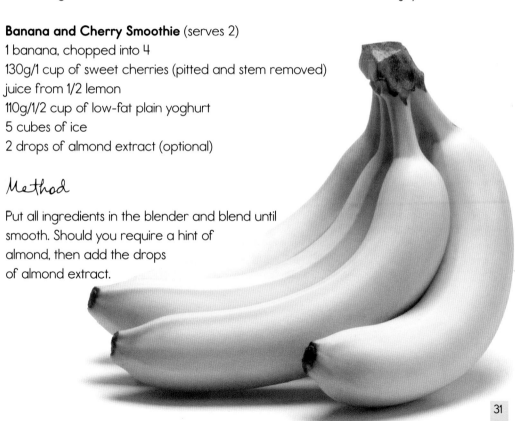

31

### Bananarama Chocoholic Smoothie (serves 2)

1 banana
2 good scoops of chocolate ice cream
6 squares of milk or dark chocolate
150ml/2/3 cup of milk

## Method

Chop the banana into four pieces then add to the blender. Add the remaining ingredients and blend until desired consistency, pour into glasses and serve.

### Banana and Chocolate Smoothie (serves 2) .

1 banana
1 tablespoon chocolate syrup
1 medium cup of milk
1 medium cup of crushed ice

## Method

Chop the banana into four pieces then add to the blender. Then add the chocolate syrup, milk and crushed ice. Blend until smooth. Pour into glasses and serve.

**Banana and Coconut Smoothie** (serves 2)

1 tablespoon of coconut milk
1/2 banana, chopped into cubes
110ml/1/2 cup of apple juice
1/2 teaspoon of fresh ginger root
2 small ice cubes or 1/2 cup crushed ice

## Method

Add all ingredients to blender and process until smooth.

**Banana and Crunchie Smoothie** (serves 2)

2 bananas
2 scoops of vanilla ice-cream
110ml/1/2 cup of milk (any type)
1 Cadburys crunchie (roughly chopped)

## Method

Add the milk and crunchie to blender. Blast them for 15 seconds, then add ice cream and bananas, blend for another 15 seconds.

**Banana Delight Smoothie** (serves 2)

2 bananas
1 tablespoon of Greek yoghurt
1 large teaspoon of Nutella
1 handful of crushed ice
275ml/1/2 pint of milk

## Method

Chop bananas then add them and all remaining ingredients to the blender. Blend, pour and enjoy. You can always add more Nutella to taste.

**Banana and Forest Berry Smoothie** (serves 2)

1 medium sized banana
115g/1 cup of frozen or fresh forest fruits
225ml/1 cup of apple juice

## Method

Place all ingredients into a blender and blend until smooth.

**Banana Hazelnut Smoothie** (serves 4)
4 medium bananas, peeled and sliced into 1/2 inch pieces
6 tablespoons light brown sugar
30g/1/4 cup hazelnuts
225ml/1 cup ice cubes
55ml/1/4 cup milk
2 tablespoons chopped hazelnuts, for garnish (optional)

## Method

Place the sliced bananas in a sealed plastic bag and put them in the freezer for 1 hour. Place the brown sugar and the hazelnuts in a blender and grind together until fine. Place the frozen bananas, ice cubes and milk in the blender with the sugar and nut mixture. Garnish with chopped nuts, if desired.

**Banana Island Smoothie** (serves 2)
55ml/1/4 cup milk
110g/1/2 cup strawberry yoghurt
55ml/1/4 cup crushed ice
1 banana (chopped)
1/2 teaspoon honey
225ml/1 cup pineapple chunks

## Method

Put all ingredients into the blend (except for the honey). Blend for approx. 20 seconds, then add the honey and whirl for a further 10 seconds.

**Banana Jungle Power Smoothie** (serves 2)
1 chopped banana, papaya and mango
225ml/1 cup of milk

## Method

Blend all of the ingredients together with 110ml/1/2 cup of ice and serve chilled.

**Banana and Mango Smoothie** (serves 1)
2 bananas
1 large mango
110ml/1/2 cup of milk

## Method

Blend all ingredients together until the mixture is smooth. This recipe can be frozen and served as a pudding for kids.

**Banana Mania Smoothie** (serves 1)
2 bananas
6 strawberries
5 raspberries
1 clementine

## Method

Blend the fruits together first, then gradually add 2 ice cubes and blend until smooth.

**Banana and Melon Crush Smoothie** (serves 2)

1 banana chopped into 4
2 good slices of melon (cubed)
2 good scoops of vanilla ice cream
splash of cranberry juice

## Method

Put the melon and banana into the blender, blast for 20 seconds.
Next, add the splash of cranberry juice and ice cream and blend
again for around 20 seconds until smooth.

**Banana and Mixed Berry Smoothie** (serves 1)

30g/1/4 cup of fresh or frozen assorted berries
1 small banana, chopped into 4
225ml/1 cup of orange juice
4 tablespoons of low fat vanilla yoghurt

## Method

Place all ingredients in the blender, blend until smooth.

**Banana and Oat Smoothie** (serves 1)
1 large or 2 small bananas
215ml/7fl oz ice cold milk
1 tablespoon rolled porridge oats
2 ice cubes

Method

Place all ingredients into the blender, mix for approximately 30 seconds.

**Banana and Orange Smoothie** (serves 1)
1 banana
225ml/1 cup of milk
225ml/1 cup of orange/pineapple juice

Method

Chop banana into 4 pieces then place all ingredients into the blender, mix for approximately 30 seconds.

## Banana Peach Smoothie (serves 1)

1 small banana, or half a large banana
60g/1/2 cup unsweetened canned peaches, drained
225ml/1 cup milk

## Method

Blend all ingredients together with 110ml/1/2 cup of ice cubes until smooth.

## Banana and Peanut Butter Smoothie (serves 2)

1 large banana, chopped into 4
335ml/1 1/2 medium size cups of milk
2 tablespoons peanut butter

## Method

Place all ingredients into the blender, blend until thick and smooth. Serve and enjoy.

## Banana and Pineapple Smoothie (serves 2)

2 large ripe bananas
4 tablespoons low fat natural yoghurt
250ml/1 1/5 cup pineapple juice

## Method

Cut the bananas into small pieces and put in the blender. Add the pineapple juice, then the low fat natural yoghurt. Blend until smooth.

**Banana Split Smoothies** (serves 2)

2 medium ripe bananas
1 can (225g/8 oz) crushed pineapple, drained
335ml/1 1/2 cups milk
60g/1/2 cup fresh or frozen unsweetened sliced strawberries
2 tablespoons honey
5 ice cubes
whipped topping, chocolate syrup & maraschino cherries

*Method*

In a blender, combine first five ingredients; cover and process until smooth. Gradually add ice, blending until slushy. Pour into chilled glasses. Garnish with whipped topping, chocolate syrup, and cherries.

**Banana and Strawberry Smoothie** (serves 2)

1 large banana
12 large strawberries
6-10 cubes of ice
sprig of mint

*Method*

Chop the banana into 4 pieces, then put them in the blender together with the strawberries and ice cubes. Blend until smooth. Serve in a tall glass and decorate with the mint.

**Banana and Strawberry Burst Smoothie** (serves 1)
1 large banana, chopped into 4 and 5 strawberries cut into halves
225ml/1 cup of milk
165g/3/4 cup of yoghurt

## Method

Place all ingredients into the blender with ice cubes, mix for approximately 30 seconds.

**Banana Sweetie Smoothie** (serves 2)
1 whole banana
30ml/1fl oz strawberry syrup
60ml/2fl oz milk

## Method

Place the banana in blender, then add 110ml/1/2 cup of crushed ice, syrup then the milk.

**Banana Toffee Smoothie** (serves 2)
2 large bananas, quartered
1 low fat toffee yoghurt
1 medium sized cup of milk

## Method

Add the bananas to the blender, next add the yoghurt then the milk, mix for about 20 seconds. Serve and enjoy!

**Kiwi Tang Smoothie** (serves 2)

60g/1/2 cup of fresh diced kiwi
60g/1/2 cup of lime sherbet
115g/1 cup of diced ripe banana
115g/1 cup of diced honeydew melon

## Method

Put all ingredients in the blender then blend until smooth.

**Kiwi Dream Smoothie** (serves 1)

150ml/2/3 cup milk
juice of 2 limes
2 kiwi fruit, peeled and chopped
1 tablespoon sugar
450ml/2 cups vanilla ice cream

## Method

Add the milk, lime juice, sugar and ice cream and blend until mixed and smooth. Then add the kiwi fruit and process until smooth.

## Green Fruit Smoothie (serves 2)

2 peeled kiwi fruits
approx 25 frozen green grapes, halved
1 frozen green apple, sliced
4-5 ice cubes
orange/apple juice to smooth it out

## Method

Put all the ingredients in blender including some juice. Blend. Add more juice if necessary.

## Kiwi, Lemon and Melon Burst Smoothie (serves 2)

2 peeled kiwi fruits
60g/1/2 cup of diced honeydew melon
110g/1/2 cup of low fat lemon yoghurt
115g/1 cup frozen green grapes
1 tablespoon of chopped fresh mint
fresh lemon juice to taste (if preferred)

## Method

Put the kiwi, honeydew melon and lemon yoghurt in a blender. Next add the grapes and mint then blend until smooth. Taste and add lemon juice if you like.

**Mango and Ginger Smoothie** (serves 2)
225g/8oz low fat vanilla yoghurt
225ml/1 cup of non-fat buttermilk
2 pieces of crystallized ginger (approx. 1 oz)
2 ripe mangos, peeled and chopped into small pieces
110ml/1/2 cup of crushed ice

## Method

In the blender purée the fruit and ginger, scraping down the sides as necessary. Add the buttermilk, yoghurt and ice and purée until smooth and frothy. Add crushed ice. Serve chilled.

**Mango Lassi Smoothie** (serves 4)
2 mangos
2 tablespoons of Greek yoghurt
55ml/1/4 pint of milk

Method

Blend the mangos, yoghurt, milk and 225ml/1 cup of ice until smooth.

**Mango Madness Smoothie** (serves 2)
450g/2 cups of low-fat vanilla yoghurt
225ml/1 cup mango nectar
2 mangos, peeled and chopped
1/4 teaspoon of cardamom

Method

Place all ingredients into blender, and process until smooth.

**Mango Pineapple Breeze Smoothie** (serves 2)
340ml/12fl oz can of frozen orange juice concentrate
170ml/6fl oz of mango premium nectar
225ml/1 cup of pineapple juice
225ml/1 cup of ice cubes

Method

Place all ingredients into blender, and process until smooth.

**Mango Squeeze Smoothie** (serves 2)
2 grapefruits
1 mango

## Method

Place the fruits into a blender with 6 ice cubes, and blend until smooth.

**Morning Burst Smoothie** (serves 1)
1 orange
1 banana
1 apple (peeled and cored)
2-3 tablespoons orange juice concentrate
ice cubes and water for texture

## Method

Cut all fruit into small chunks, place in blender. Next add water and orange juice concentrate, then blend for approx 20-30 seconds adding ice for texture as desired.

**Orange Aniseed Twist Smoothie** (serves 2)
3 oranges
2 sticks of celery (each chopped into 4 pieces)
1/4 fennel bulb

## Method

Place all ingredients into blender, and mix for approximately 30 seconds then serve.

**Peach and Orange Smoothie** (serves 2)
1/2 tin of peaches
2 tablespoons of natural yoghurt
250-400ml/1-2 cups of fresh orange juice

## Method

Open the tin of peaches and put half of the peaches into the blender (pour approx two thirds of the syrup in also). Next, add the natural yoghurt. Finally add between 250-400ml/1-2 cups of the orange juice depending on preference. Blend well, serve and enjoy.

**Pineapple and Banana Smoothie** (serves 2)
2 large ripe bananas
4 tablespoons low fat natural yoghurt
225ml/1 cup pineapple juice

## Method

Cut the bananas into small pieces and put in the blender.
Add the pineapple juice, then the low fat natural
yoghurt. Blend until smooth.

**Strawberry Cherry Berry Smoothie** (serves 4)
345g/3 cups frozen pitted dark sweet cherries
345g/3 cups frozen whole strawberries
675ml/3 cups cranberry juice

## Method

In a blender, puree half the frozen pitted dark sweet cherries, half the frozen strawberries and half the cranberry juice, stirring as needed, until smooth. Pour into two serving glasses. Repeat with remaining ingredients for two more servings.

**Strawberry Margarita Smoothie** (serves 2)

15 strawberries
2 cups of crushed ice
2/3 cup margarita mixer
2 shots tequilla
1 tablespoon orange juice concentrate
2 teaspoons sweetened lime juice

## Method

Put strawberries in a blender, then add margarita mixer, tequilla, orange juice concentrate and sweetened lime juice, add crushed ice on top. Blend until nearly smooth. Pour into 2 glasses and garnish with whole strawberries.

**Strawberry Multi-Fruit Yoghurt Smoothie** (serves 1)

half ripe mango
6 fresh/frozen strawberries
1 banana
1 small apple
5 tablespoons strawberry yoghurt
5 ice cubes

## Method

Peel and chunk all the fruit and put in blender, add yoghurt then ice cubes. Blend for approx 40 seconds till smooth.

**Strawberry, Orange and Kiwi Smoothie** (serves 2)
250g/9oz fresh strawberries
300ml/1 1/3 cups pure orange juice
2 kiwi fruit, peeled and core removed
1 teaspoon of honey (optional)
1 halved strawberry and 2 slices of peeled kiwi fruit to decorate the glass

Method

Blend all ingredients until smooth. Decorate the glasses, then serve.

**Strawberry Orange Splash Smoothie** (serves 2)
10 strawberries (save 2 for garnish)
1 medium sized cup of fresh orange juice
1/4 orange
6 ice cubes

Method

Chop 8 strawberries in halves. Peel and slice the 1/4 of orange, put all the ingredients in a blender and mix until smooth. Pour into 2 glasses and garnish with a strawberry in each.

**Berry Fruity Smoothie** (serves 2)
25g/1/4 cup raspberries
75ml/1/3 cup of non-fat, sugar free vanilla yoghurt
225ml/1 cup of orange juice
1 small banana, chop into 4 pieces

## Method

Chop the banana into 4 pieces, then place all ingredients in the blender and blend until smooth.

**Berry and Mango Blast Smoothie** (serves 4)                **Alcoholic**
1 whole mango
1/2 punnet of strawberries
1/2 punnet of raspberries
1 large cup of ice cubes
2 shots of vodka

## Method

Blend altogether until the ice is nearly gone.

**Blueberry and Pineapple Smoothie** (serves 2)

230g/2 cups of chilled fresh or frozen blueberries, slightly thawed
225ml/1 cup of chilled pineapple or orange juice
225g/8oz carton of low-fat vanilla yoghurt
1 tablespoon of sugar

Method

In a blender, combine all ingredients. Cover and blend for between 1-2 minutes until nearly smooth.

**Blueberry and Yoghurt Smoothie** (serves 1)

60g/1/2 cup of wild blueberries
110g/1/2 cup of blueberry yoghurt
1/2 a banana
3 cubes of ice

Method

Blend the banana, ice and yoghurt together until the banana is well blended. Add the blueberries and blend on low speed for 30 seconds. Adding the blueberries at the end leaves the blueberry flavour at the top.

**Strawberry Shot Smoothie** (serves 2)
170ml/6fl oz orange juice
60ml/2fl oz milk
1 peeled and frozen banana
3 to 5 frozen strawberries
1 fresh peeled peach
1/2 teaspoon cinnamon

## Method

Put all in a blender and whip at high speed until smooth. Pour into two glasses.

**Strawberry Slushy Smoothie** (serves 1)
4 large strawberries
1 teaspoon of sugar
110ml/1/2 cup of whole milk
225ml/1 cup of ice cubes

## Method

Blend strawberries with milk on low speed till smooth, then add ice cubes and blend on high. Add sugar and blend on high speed for about 1 minute. The texture should be slushy and smooth.

**Strawberry and Raspberry Smoothie** (serves 2)
230g/2 cups of frozen strawberries and raspberries
75ml/1/3 cup of milk
2 teaspoons of honey
2 scoops of vanilla ice cream
175g/6 oz of yoghurt

## Method

Place everything in the blender. Blend for approximately 20 seconds, serve and enjoy.

**Strawberry and Watermelon Smoothie** (serves 2)
150g/1 1/5 cup strawberries
1/8 of a watermelon

## Method

Put watermelon and strawberries into the blender (keeping two strawberries aside for decoration), blend for approximately 20 seconds. Pour into two glasses and garnish each glass with a strawberry on a cocktail stick.

## Strawberry Summer Sun Smoothie (serves 2)

2 kiwis
half a punnet of strawberries
2 apples
1 large orange

### Method

Chop each piece of fruit up into reasonably small pieces then put into the blender. Blend until your desired consistency. Serve.

## Strawberry Sweetie Smoothie (serves 2)

6 large strawberries
30ml/1fl oz strawberry syrup
60ml/2fl oz milk
110ml/1/2 cup of cubed or crushed ice

### Method

Place the strawberries in blender, then add the ice, syrup then the milk.

## Strawberry and Banana Yoghurt Smoothie (serves 2)

165ml/3/4 cup apple juice
110g/1/2 cup natural yoghurt
1 banana, sliced and frozen
115g/1 cup frozen strawberries

### Method

Pour the apple juice into a blender. Add the yoghurt and process until smooth. Add the frozen banana slices and half of the strawberries and process well, then add the remaining strawberries and process until smooth.

## Strawberry and Cranberry Smoothie (serves 2)

225ml/8fl oz cranberry juice
5 strawberries cut into halves
5 ice cubes

### Method

Place all ingredients into blender, and process until smooth.

smoothies

**Summer Smoothie** (serves 2)
150g/1 1/5 cup strawberries (tops off)
10g/1/4 oz raspberries
2 chopped and peeled apples
2 bananas
1 small cup of pineapple juice
55g/1/3 cup natural yoghurt
1 small cup of crushed ice

## Method

Add the strawberries and raspberries to the blender, next add the pineapple juice, apples, bananas, yoghurt then the ice. Mix for 30-40 seconds.

**Summer Red Smoothie** (serves 2)
8 large strawberries
1/2 banana
1 orange
3 pineapple slices
1 medium cup of pure apple juice
1 medium cup of crushed ice

## Method

Put all ingredients (except ice) in blender and blend for approx. 30 seconds. Next add the ice and blend until your preferred texture. Serve immediately for best results. Perfect for hot Summer days!

**Passion Fruit and Strawberry Chill** (serves 2)
handful of frozen strawberries and 1 chopped banana
150ml/2/3 cup yoghurt (mango papaya and passionfruit is best)
200ml/4/5 cup passion fruit juice

## Method

Mix in the smoothie maker until smooth.

**Peachy Banana Smoothie** (serves 2)
1 medium sized tin of peaches
1 large banana
1 small cup of fresh orange juice

## Method

Break up the banana and put in your blender. Next add the tin of peaches (drained of syrup) and enough orange juice to cover your banana pieces. Blend and enjoy.

**Orange Mango Smoothie** (serves 2)
175g/1 1/2 small cups of chopped mango
450ml/2 cups of fresh orange juice
2 tablespoons of sugar

## Method

Blend all the ingredients in the blender and blend until desired consistency.

**Orange Delight Smoothie** (serves 4)
180ml/6fl oz can frozen orange juice concentrate
225ml/1 cup of water
225ml/1 cup of skimmed milk
1 teaspoon of vanilla extract
10 ice cubes

## Method

Place all of the ingredients into a blender, and process until smooth. If you do not have frozen orange juice concentrate, try adding the juice of 4 freshly squeezed oranges.

**Orange Fruity Smoothie** (serves 2)
1 banana, chopped and cut into 4
1 peach, halved, pitted and cut into cubes
1 cup raspberries
110ml/1/2 cup freshly squeezed orange juice
3 ice cubes

## Method

Place all of ingredients into a blender, and process until smooth. You can substitute orange juice for pineapple or a tropical blended juice for a more exotic flavour.

**Papaya and Raspberry Smoothie** (serves 1)

1 frozen banana, peeled
1/2 fresh papaya
10-12 raspberries (fresh or frozen)
300ml/1 1/3 cup fruit juice

## Method

Pour all of the ingredients into a blender, then whiz until a smooth consistency is reached. You can also add additional liquid if you feel the smoothie is too thick for your taste.

**Papaya, Honey and Cinnamon** (serves 1)

1 large papaya
2 tablespoons honey
cinnamon to taste
200ml/4/5 cup greek style yoghurt
handful of ice

## Method

De-stone and de-skin the papaya and then chop into chunks. Add all of the ingredients together in a blender and blend until smooth.

**Passion Fruit and Banana Smoothie** (serves 2)

1 large banana
2 passion fruit
450ml/2 cups milk
2 drops vanilla essence
3-4 ice cubes (optional)

## Method

Slice the banana, halve the passion fruits and scoop out the seeds and fruit and add to the blender. Add the milk, vanilla essence and ice cubes (if adding), and blend on high until all the ingredients are well blended.

**Passion Fruit, Mango & Pineapple Smoothie** (serves 1)

2 passion fruits, pulp only
1 small mango, cut into chunks
75g pineapple, cut into chunks
75ml pineapple juice
1 lime, juice only
7 ice cubes
a pinch of ground black pepper
a pinch of cayenne pepper (optional)

## Method

Blend all of the ingredients together until smooth. If you prefer your smoothie to have a little "kick" add a pinch of cayenne pepper.

**Pineapple and Coconut Smoothie** (serves 2)
250g/2 cups cubed/chopped pineapple
1 scoop vanilla ice cream
1/3 small cup of coconut
1 banana
2 medium cups of milk
2 ice cubes

Method

Add all ingredients to the blender. Blend for approximately 30 seconds or until desired
consistency. Serve and enjoy immediately.

**Refresher Smoothie** (serves 1)
2 good slices of fresh pineapple
2 pears (skin and centre removed)
4 strawberries
splash of juice (either orange or apple)

Method

Add all fruit into the blender and whiz for around 30 seconds. Pour and enjoy.

smoothies

**Pineapple Crush Smoothie** (serves 1)
110ml/1/2 cup pineapple juice
4 tablespoons orange juice
90g/3/4 cup melon, roughly chopped
115g/1 cup frozen pineapple chunks
4 ice cubes

## Method

Pour the pineapple juice and orange juice into a blender and process gently until combined. Add the melon, pineapple, and ice cubes and process until slushy. Pour into glasses.

**Pineapple and Melon Smoothie** (serves 2)
1/2 galia melon
4 pineapple rings
1 banana
2 tablespoons of natural yoghurt
5 ice cubes
dash of pineapple juice

## Method

Add all ingredients to the blender and put the cubes at the top. Blast for 30 seconds and serve in a long glass with a straw - lovely!

**Apple and Avocado Smoothie** (serves 2)

1 apple

1/2 ripe avocado

1/2 carton apple juice

3 ice cubes

3 sprigs mint leaves

1 teaspoon freshly squeezed lime juice

## Method

Core and cut the apple into 4 pieces then combine all the ingredients together in a blender.

**Celery & Kiwi Smoothie** (serves 2)

4 very ripe kiwis

1 ripe banana

3 stalks of celery

water

## Method

Blend all ingredients until smooth. Add water to taste.

## Spoons to millilitres

| | | | |
|---|---|---|---|
| 1/2 Teaspoon | 2.5ml | 1 Tablespoon | 15ml |
| 1 Teaspoon | 5ml | 2 Tablespoons | 30ml |
| 1-1/2 Teaspoons | 7.5ml | 3 Tablespoon | 45ml |
| 2 Teaspoons | 10 ml | 4 Tablespoons | 60ml |

## Grams to Ounces

| | | | |
|---|---|---|---|
| 10g | 0.25oz | 225g | 8oz |
| 15g | 0.38oz | 250g | 9oz |
| 25g | 1oz | 275g | 10oz |
| 50g | 2oz | 300g | 11oz |
| 75g | 3oz | 350g | 12oz |
| 110g | 4oz | 375g | 13oz |
| 150g | 5oz | 400g | 14oz |
| 175g | 6oz | 425g | 15oz |
| 200g | 7oz | 450g | 16oz |

## Metric to Cups

| Description | Metric | Cup |
|---|---|---|
| Flour etc | 115g | 1 cup |
| Clear Honey etc | 350g | 1 cup |
| Liquids | 225ml | 1 cup |

## Liquid measures

| Fl oz | Pints | ml |
|---|---|---|
| 5fl oz | 1/4 pint | 150ml |
| 7.5fl oz | | 215ml |
| 10fl oz | 1/2 pint | 275ml |
| 15fl oz | | 425ml |
| 20fl oz | 1 pint | 570ml |
| 35fl oz | 1-3/4 pints | 1 litre |

Conversion charts

89

## Nutritional Values

| Food substance = 100 g. | energy kJ/Kcal | water % | fibre g | fat g | protein g | sugar g | vit.A ug |
|---|---|---|---|---|---|---|---|
| Apple | 207/49 | 84 | 2.3 | 0 | 0.4 | 11.8 | 2 |
| Apricot | 153/36 | 87 | 2.1 | 0 | 1.0 | 8.0 | 420 |
| Avocado | 523/126 | 81 | 0.2 | 10 | 2.0 | 7.0 | 20 |
| Banana | 375/88 | 76 | 2.7 | 0 | 1.2 | 20.4 | 3 |
| Blackberry | 170/40 | 85 | 8.7 | 0 | 2.0 | 8.0 | 30 |
| Blueberry | 204/48 | 80 | 8.4 | 0 | 1.0 | 11.0 | 0 |
| Carrots | 48 /11 | 92 | 3.3 | 0 | 0.6 | 2.2 | 312 |
| Cherry | 221/52 | 86 | 1.2 | 0 | 0.0 | 13.0 | 40 |
| Cranberry | 68 /16 | 89 | 4.2 | 0 | 0.0 | 4.0 | 0 |
| Date | 1275/300 | 20 | 7.5 | 0 | 2.0 | 73.0 | 0 |
| Fig | 340/80 | 80 | 2.0 | 0 | 1.0 | 19.0 | 10 |
| Gooseberry | 170/40 | 88 | 3.2 | 0 | 1.0 | 9.0 | 0 |
| Grapefruit, Red | 128/30 | 90 | 1.4 | 0 | 0.9 | 6.6 | 0 |
| Grapes | 274/64 | 83 | 2.2 | 0 | 0.6 | 15.5 | 0 |
| Guava | 306/72 | 81 | 5.3 | 0 | 1.0 | 17.0 | 30 |
| Kiwi Fruit | 168/40 | 84 | 2.1 | 0 | 1.1 | 8.8 | 5 |
| Lemon | 51/12 | 96 | 1.8 | 0 | 0.0 | 3.0 | 0 |
| Lime | 156/37 | 91 | 0.3 | 0 | 0.0 | 7.0 | 0 |
| Lychee | 323/76 | 82 | 1.5 | 0 | 1.0 | 18.0 | 0 |
| Mandarin/Tangerine | 177/42 | 88 | 1.9 | 0 | 0.9 | 9.5 | 12 |
| Mango | 255/60 | 84 | 1.0 | 0 | 0.0 | 15.0 | 210 |

## Nutritional Values

| Food substance = 100 g. | vit.C mg | vit.B1 mg | vit.B2 mg | vit.B6 mg | vit.E mg |
|---|---|---|---|---|---|
| Apple | 15 | 0.02 | 0.01 | 0.05 | 0.5 |
| Apricot | 5 | 0.06 | 0.05 | 0.06 | 0.5 |
| Avocado | 17 | 0.06 | 0.12 | 0.36 | 3.2 |
| Banana | 10 | 0.04 | 0.03 | 0.36 | 0.3 |
| Blackberry | 150 | 0.08 | 0.04 | 0.07 | 1.0 |
| Blueberry | 10 | 0.02 | 0.03 | 0.05 | 1.9 |
| Carrots | 2 | 0.03 | 0.04 | 0.08 | 0.2 |
| Cherry | 10 | 0.02 | 0.02 | 0.04 | 0.1 |
| Cranberry | 15 | 0.00 | 0.01 | 0.07 | 0 |
| Date | 0 | 0.05 | 0.10 | 0.10 | 0.7 |
| Fig | 3 | 0.06 | 0.05 | 0.11 | 0 |
| Gooseberry | 30 | 0.02 | 0.01 | 0.08 | 0.4 |
| Grapefruit, Red | 40 | 0.07 | 0.02 | 0.03 | 0.5 |
| Grapes | 3 | 0.03 | 0.01 | 0.08 | 0.6 |
| Guava | 218 | 0.04 | 0.04 | 0.14 | 0 |
| Kiwi Fruit | 70 | 0.01 | 0.02 | 0.12 | 1.9 |
| Lemon | 40 | 0.06 | 0.02 | 0.04 | 0.8 |
| Lime | 140 | 0.03 | 0.02 | 0.08 | 0 |
| Lychee | 39 | 0.05 | 0.05 | 0 | 0 |
| Mandarin/Tangerine | 30 | 0.08 | 0.03 | 0.084 | 0.4 |
| Mango | 53 | 0.05 | 0.06 | 0.13 | 1.0 |

## Nutritional Values

| Food substance = 100 g. | energy kJ/Kcal | water % | fibre g | fat g | protein g | sugar g | vit.A ug |
|---|---|---|---|---|---|---|---|
| Melon, Red Water | 153/36 | 93 | 0.6 | 0 | 1.0 | 8.0 | 30 |
| Melon, Cantaloupe | 122/29 | 89 | 0.6 | 0 | 0.9 | 6.3 | 7 |
| Orange | 198/47 | 87 | 1.8 | 0 | 1.0 | 10.6 | 2 |
| Papaya | 136/32 | 91 | 0.6 | 0 | 0.0 | 8.0 | 40 |
| Passion Fruit | 158/37 | 88 | 3.3 | 0.4 | 2.6 | 5.8 | 125 |
| Peach | 151/36 | 89 | 1.4 | 0 | 1.0 | 7.9 | 15 |
| Pear | 201/47 | 86 | 2.1 | 0 | 0.3 | 11.5 | 0.0 |
| Red Bell Pepper | 119/28 | 91 | 2.2 | 0 | 1.0 | 6.0 | 172 |
| Pineapple | 211/50 | 84 | 1.2 | 0 | 0.4 | 12.0 | 20 |
| Pomegranate | 343/81 | 82 | 3.4 | 0 | 1.0 | 17.0 | 10 |
| Plum | 177/42 | 84 | 2.2 | 0 | 0.8 | 9.6 | 18 |
| Strawberry | 99/23 | 91 | 2.2 | 0 | 0.7 | 5.1 | 10 |
| Tomato | 48/11 | 97 | 1.4 | 0 | 0.9 | 1.9 | 140 |

## Nutritional Values

| Food substance = 100 g. | vit.C mg | vit.B1 mg | vit.B2 mg | vit.B6 mg | vit.E mg |
|---|---|---|---|---|---|
| Melon, Red Water | 6 | 0.04 | 0.05 | 0.07 | 0 |
| Melon, Cantaloupe | 32 | 0.05 | 0.02 | 0.10 | 0.2 |
| Orange | 49 | 0.07 | 0.03 | 0.06 | 0.1 |
| Papaya | 46 | 0.03 | 0.04 | 0.04 | 0 |
| Passion Fruit | 123 | 0.03 | 0.12 | 0 | 0.5 |
| Peach | 7 | 0.01 | 0.02 | 0.02 | 0.0 |
| Pear | 4 | 0.01 | 0.01 | 0.02 | 0.1 |
| Red Bell Pepper | 80 | 0.04 | 0.14 | 0.43 | 6.4 |
| Pineapple | 25 | 0.07 | 0.02 | 0.09 | 0.1 |
| Pomegranate | 7 | 0.05 | 0.02 | 0.31 | 0 |
| Plum | 5 | 0.02 | 0.03 | 0.10 | 0.7 |
| Strawberry | 60 | 0.02 | 0.03 | 0.06 | 0.4 |
| Tomato | 15 | 0.05 | 0.02 | 0.08 | 0.7 |

Source: Nevo table 1996, Nevo Foundation, Netherlands Nutrition Centre

# Index of Recipes

Index of Recipes

**Publishers Disclaimer**

This edition published in 2008 by Bizzybee Publishing Ltd.
© bizzybee publishing 2008 Printed in China